In 1998, I was 35 years old, wishing I could retire so I could find and live out my calling in life. The corporate career I had educated myself for and worked hard to achieve no longer held any joy for me. On the surface, I had it all—nice salary, benefits, big office, promising future. Deep down, I felt my life was wasting away.

Not to say that working in the corporate world is somehow without any joy or contrary to God's will. Hardly. Some of the most devout Christians I know work in the marketplace. God has called and equipped them, and they take great joy in serving Christ through their work.

During the first 13 years of my working career (public accounting and later the insurance industry), I knew I was right where God wanted me, and I took great joy in contributing to the success of the companies I worked for and helping their clients. But something changed. It came out of left field and turned my world upside down. I began to feel discontent, uninspired and empty in my employment. Little did I know God was moving me toward a new chapter in my life.

Through the concepts I've learned and included in this book, I found my next calling in life. Not a higher calling or one more worthy than my previous corporate position. Rather, one where I am again joyful having found God's next assignment for me in life. Now, I don't even think about retirement. Slowing down someday, sure, but why would I want to quit what I so enjoy?

My next calling was to inner-city youth ministry, the furthest thing from my mind. Yet God allowed me to be a part of His plan to rescue hundreds of at-risk and homeless youth with the gospel of Jesus Christ through the formation of a ministry called Freedom for Youth Ministries.

The purpose of this study guide is twofold, 1) To help believers discover and live out their God-given purpose in life, which will bring untold joy, and 2) To equip and send laborers into the harvest field. For Jesus said, *"The harvest is plentiful, but the workers are few. Ask the Lord of the harvest, therefore, to send out workers into his harvest field." (Matthew 9:37-38)*

Every church and mission, local or global, needs more workers to bring in the harvest. It's what we as Christians are created to do in our own unique way. And the fulfillment is greater than anything the world has to offer. Get ready for an encounter with God—your life may never be the same!

Mark Nelson, Freedom for Youth Ministries

Freedom for Youth Ministries is offering this study guide at a nominal price to maximize its distribution while covering the printing costs. Any profits from the sale of this study guide will go to Freedom for Youth to advance its programs to distressed and impoverished youth in Iowa.

FOR JESUS SAID,

"The **HARVEST IS PLENTIFUL**, but the **WORKERS ARE FEW**. Ask the Lord of the harvest, therefore, to send out workers into his harvest field."

Matthew 9:37-38

Introduction

Maybe you attend church weekly, belong to a small group or are part of a regular Bible study. You pray most every day and try your best to live out your faith at home and at work. Still, you feel like there's something missing. Once in awhile you can't help but wonder, "Am I experiencing the fullness in life that Jesus came to give me?" *(John 10:10)*

Wouldn't it be terrible to find out at the end of your life that you missed something that was the key to unlocking great amounts of joy and peace? What if you realized you were looking in all the wrong places? What if your life was full of worry because you just couldn't find peace in the storms of life, most of which never amounted to a raindrop?

This book is on experiencing a new level of joy and fullness in life, a feeling of completeness. It's where life makes sense and you've never felt closer to God. Through this study, you will begin to experience a greater depth of God's love. Feelings of peace will dispel your deepest worries. Somehow, you'll just know God has it all worked out.

This happens when you find your calling in life—those activities that God has orchestrated just for you to do. Your focus shifts to someone else, and you get more than you give, yet you don't know how. It's God's formula for joy that defies logic.

Let's face it; time is a commodity that's hard to give up. It's an asset that has limited duration. We can't invest it and earn more, or save it to use later. Our obligations of work, family, household chores, etc. often leave us with precious little time to spare, and even less energy to use what's left productively.

Your life may be fast-paced with school activities, a demanding job or teenagers involved in every sport. Some of you may be just the opposite—your nest is empty; maybe you're retired and you're wondering how to live life to the fullest with the years you have left.

Don't worry; this study will not try to convince you to quit your job that pays the bills or make you feel guilty because you spend time and money doing a hobby you really enjoy. God wants that for you. In fact, He'll make it even better. Nor is this study a message that just serving others produces a lifetime of bliss. Life's not that easy. It's more about balance—family, work, play and serving others, all under the umbrella of living as a follower of Jesus Christ.

If you've found your calling and life is hitting on all cylinders for you, enjoy this study series as a way to help others in your group find theirs. Share your journey of how God led you to your calling and how it has enriched your life. God may also show you the next step in your faith journey, because our callings develop and change over time. However, if you're like the vast majority of Christians, there's still a hidden pearl waiting for you to discover. Finding your calling will satisfy your soul and draw you closer to God as you align yourself to His will.

For those who have found the pearl, life has never been the same. You know who they are. Troubles in life don't seem to concern them as much anymore. They're focused on the big picture. They've rearranged their priorities in life, without even noticing, and their relationships with others have become more meaningful to them. Worship and Bible study have more significance now for them, and their prayer life has grown deeper. They've found true meaning in life, and it gives them great peace.

This study series will help you understand why it's worth the effort to find your niche in God's vast kingdom, and show you simple steps on how to find it. Unlike writings that focus on discovering your spiritual gifts, this study will help you find your passion, that which God has placed in your heart. Once you know whom you will serve, you will naturally be drawn to those activities that suit your spiritual gifts.

That's not to say that finding your calling is easy. It takes patience, some concerted effort, and mostly, a listening ear. As you study the text, ponder the questions, and openly share within your small group, you can expect the Holy Spirit to show up and guide you to a more rewarding and fulfilling life.

TABLE of CONTENTS

Why Should I Take Time to Discover My Calling?

It's a good question. Maybe one you wouldn't ask in your group. However, the rest of the study series will have little value until you resolve this question. You have to be fully convinced that discovering and living out your God-given calling brings you closer to your Creator. It brings balance and harmony and helps you enjoy more fully every aspect of your life—career, hobbies and spending time with loved ones, all of which are ordained by your Creator. Without that serving element in your life, the thing God has specifically created you to do, you can never really grasp your purpose in life, which leads to completeness and fulfillment.

The following questions may help bring clarity to how God is steering you to your calling. (Feel free to jot down some notes, as you'll have an opportunity to discuss these questions further in your small group.)

1) Deep in your soul, do you sense that something is missing in your life? It's hard to pinpoint, but you've learned through experience that nothing in this world can satisfy this longing, not the security of wealth, titles, achievements, possessions, travel or even family and friends.

2) Do you find yourself wanting to grow deeper in your faith, but you don't know how? Maybe your Bible study time has diminished to the point where you do it occasionally to avoid guilt. Your prayers lack passion and conviction. Worship time at church may even feel uninspiring or lifeless.

3) Do you occasionally have a vision or dream that brings you much excitement? Maybe a mission trip to Africa, housing homeless mothers with children, starting a worship service at a nursing home; the possibilities are endless. You usually think about it when you have some time alone away from your regular schedule; maybe on vacation. It may be too big to talk about or you've placed it on the back burner until you're financially secure or have more time.

4) Do your pursuits in life have eternal consequences, or will they die when you do? In other words, do you think about "storing up treasures in heaven" or are you living for this world? (Matthew 6:20)

The Example of Cornelius

Let's take a look at one man in the Bible who found his calling and see how it impacted his life and how God used him to help change the world.

Cornelius was a Roman Centurion (in charge of 100 men) shortly after Jesus' resurrection. His status as a Roman officer surely brought much power, respect and income. Yet the Bible says, *"He and all his family were devout and God-fearing; he gave generously to those in need and prayed to God regularly. One day he was visited by an angel of God who said to Cornelius, 'Your prayers and gifts to the poor have come up as a memorial offering before God.'"* (Acts 10:1-4)

Can you imagine being told by an angel that your prayers and service have been placed at the throne of God as a memorial offering? God recognizes our service unto Him, and it gives Him much delight. Maybe no one notices that you arrive before dawn every Sunday at your church to help cook breakfast, but God does. And it gives Him much joy.

Cornelius, more than likely, faced many of the same pressures we face today—achieving a higher rank, perhaps a higher standard of living, or the power of managing many people. But Cornelius had found true joy in his prayer life and giving to the poor. There was satisfaction and contentment in knowing he was doing what he was called to, and it pleased his heavenly Father.

Jesus said, "Where your treasure is, there your heart will be also." *(Matthew 6:21)*. Cornelius had a calling in his heart to help the poor. And his treasure followed. Undoubtedly, his "generous giving" included acts of love and kindness to those he served. He surely knew the names of the poor in his community, where they came from, and how he could pray for them. That's what happens when you find your passion. It isn't just writing a check. For Cornelius it was a purpose in life. Maybe leading Roman soldiers was also part of his calling, or maybe he realized that his job allowed him to take care of his family and serve the poor. Nonetheless, he discovered real meaning in life, and his obedience to his calling was an offering to God, something that pleased our heavenly Father.

God sees our works, and when done with the right motive in obedience to our calling, they are memorial offerings to Him. Our obedience also opens future opportunities to be used by God. As recorded in Acts chapter 10, God used Cornelius in a powerful way to show Peter that he was no longer under the law as a Jew and that the new covenant was also for Gentiles. Peter brought salvation through the gospel of Jesus Christ to Cornelius and his family.

You Were Created to Serve

"For we are God's workmanship, created in Christ Jesus, to do good works that He prepared in advance for us to do." (Ephesians 2:10)

We are God's workmanship—His work of artistry. You are a one-of-a-kind masterpiece that was created to carry out God's work. Our skills are not man-made but formed in us through Christ Jesus for a purpose. Our purpose, that which God prepared for us before we were born, is our calling in life, or our mission.

To Serve is to Love

Jesus said, "A new command I give you: Love one another. As I have loved you, so you must love one another. By this everyone will know that you are my disciples, if you love one another." (John 13:34-35)

Be assured that your calling is going to involve loving others. Even acts of generosity that appear to have little human interaction, such as mowing your church lawn or doing bookkeeping for your favorite ministry, are acts of love. Jesus displayed His love for us through service (such as washing the disciple's feet) and sacrifice, paid with his shed blood on the cross at Calvary. It's how we should love others, selflessly and sacrificially. Our desire should be to follow Jesus' commandment because we love Him. We love because He first loved us. *(1 John 4:19)* We demonstrate our love for our Savior through obeying His command to love others through service and sacrifice, namely following our call. Three times Jesus asked Peter if he loved Him, and three times Peter affirmed that he did. Each time Jesus responded by commanding Peter to *"feed his sheep." (John 21:15-17)*

In other words, Jesus was telling Peter to demonstrate his love for Him by carrying out his calling.

Joy Comes Through Obedience

"If you obey my commands, you will remain in my love, just as I have obeyed my Father's commands and remain in His love. I have told you this so that my joy may be in you and your joy may be complete." (John 15:10-11)

Our labor of love to carry out our calling in life is rewarded with Jesus' promise that we will have His joy and that joy in us will be complete. We will be in harmony with our Creator's purpose, and that will bring us completeness, contentment and unspeakable joy. This is why you find people who are always joyful in spite of their circumstances in life. They're not chasing something they can never obtain nor seeking happiness through the world, which always ends in disappointment. They have no worries of lying on their deathbed full of regrets or belaboring the sacrifices they made to obtain worldly treasures that now mean nothing.

Answering our calling reflects our obedience to our Maker. To not carry out the works He gave us to do is to reject His calling, which leads to emptiness, separation and discontent.

"And I saw that all labor and all achievement spring from man's envy of his neighbor. This too is meaningless, a chasing after the wind." Ecclesiastes 4:4

A Lesson in Wisdom

As King Solomon, the wisest man on Earth, declared, *"My heart took delight in all my work, and this was the reward for all my labor. Yet when I surveyed all that my hands had done and what I had toiled to achieve, everything was meaningless, a chasing after the wind; nothing was gained under the sun."* He further writes, *"And I saw that all labor and all achievement spring from man's envy of his neighbor. This too is meaningless, a chasing after the wind." (Ecclesiastes 2:11, 4:4)*

Solomon realized that working for personal achievements, outside of God's calling for our lives, is meaningless. What if we all put down our personal agendas and strived to find those things God created us to do? Some would love the orphan boy and raise him to become a mighty man of God instead of someday being locked away in prison, leaving behind victims of his crime. Others would take care of the widow and the disabled instead of delegating this to the government. Wealth would be planted in the Kingdom of God, feeding the starving people in Third World countries, starting churches, and providing relief for the oppressed, instead of passing it down to the next generation to be consumed.

Regardless of where you are in life, it's not too late to find your niche in God's plan to redeem the world. You can leave behind a legacy that produces fruit for generations to come in the Kingdom of God. You can

"When I am living out my calling, I feel stronger in my walk with Christ and as a man. There is an intrinsic reward in giving and serving."

Rick Williams (Retired school teacher, mentor for inner-city high school youth)

be the light of Jesus Christ to a lost and dying world and watch God do miraculous things through you; things you never imagined.

Hopefully, you're convinced that finding your calling in life, that which God has appointed and equipped you for, is worth the time to pursue. Unfortunately, far too many Christians have passed on, leaving God's work for them unfinished.

Are you ready to get started? Are you tired of focusing your energy on things that are temporal rather than eternal? A whole new world awaits those who would dare to seek God's heart for the things He has ordained for them to do. Let's go!

PART 1

1) Discuss with your group the questions on page 7. How have any of the questions stirred your heart to find your calling in life or pursue additional things God may have for you to do?

_____

_____

_____

_____

_____

2) Are there things in your life that are crowding out your ability to serve?

_____

_____

_____

_____

_____

3) What steps can you take now to free up time or resources to invest in things that are eternal rather than temporal?

_____

_____

_____

_____

_____

discussion questions continued on pg 14

4) *Write your own eulogy. In other words, what would you want a family member or close friend to say about you at your funeral when you're gone? Don't be afraid of sounding prideful or conceited; remember, you're gone! If you're comfortable, you can share it with your group or just keep it to yourself. Discuss as a group how this exercise allowed you to gain perspective in your life.*

5) What are the things you are pursuing in life now that really wouldn't be important to include in your eulogy?

_____

_____

_____

_____

_____

_____

6) What are the things you know you need to do and that you hope will be a part of your eulogy?

_____

_____

_____

_____

_____

_____

_____

_____

_____

_____

_____

Part 2

Discovering My Calling in Life

If you're feeling a little uneasy after chapter one, don't worry. The Holy Spirit may be getting your attention. God loves you and wants what's best for you. Feelings of condemnation, guilt or fear are from the enemy. *"Therefore, there is now no condemnation in Christ Jesus." (Romans 8:1)*

If the steps that you feel are necessary to answer your call seem impossible or contrary to the world, you're in good company. Everyone who accepts God's assignments faces resistance. Even if it's giving two hours of your time a week or giving away your year-end bonus, in your mind there are a thousand reasons why you shouldn't do it. You are experiencing the process of dying to yourself. And what will follow will bring a wellspring of joy and peace.

Maybe you have an idea of where God wants to use you; however, more than likely, you're just not sure. If you're serious about this, it's time to seek God's heart. Find your prayer closest and turn off your phone; if you don't, you are sure to be interrupted. Establish a routine prayer life, including in your prayers a request that God would reveal to you His calling for your life. Read your Bible, again asking God to speak to you through His Word. God promises that if we ask, it will be given to us; if we seek, we will find; and if we knock, the door will be opened. *(Matthew 7:7)* Meditate on scripture that grabs your attention. Memorize it. Write a verse each day on an index card and review the cards daily. Before long, you will have the Word of God planted deep in your heart, and a protective armor to guard you in spiritual battles. Throughout the day, ask God to direct you.

This time of seeking God's heart will grow your faith, which is exactly what He wants from you before He can send you out. To skip (or discontinue) building your relationship with God will cause you to steer off course. A loving God would never give an assignment to one of His children before they were ready. He wants you to succeed. To hear God's voice, we must know Him intimately; and to know Him intimately, we must commune with Him daily through prayer and reading his Word.

In your time with God, maybe an idea has come to your mind or you've seen an opportunity to give of your time and/or resources to love others in advancing the Kingdom. How can you be sure? Let's look at Gideon.

Gideon's Example

Gideon was a mighty warrior in charge of Israel's army. When asked by God to go into battle against the superior Midianite army with just 300 soldiers armed with trumpets, Gideon asked God for confirmation. Gideon put out a wool fleece on the ground to confirm that what he was hearing was really from God. If the fleece had dew on it in the morning and the ground was dry, he knew God would save Israel in battle. In the morning, it happened just as he requested. He confirmed it again, this time asking God to not put dew on the fleece but on the ground. Again, it happened. Gideon was obedient, and God defeated the enemy. *(Judges 6-7)*

Although the decisions facing you are probably not life and death as Gideon's were, it's logical to expect God to show us signs as we search, or put out our fleece. Start with your church. Find the list of volunteer opportunities available and the time commitments and expectations for each. Get a list of the Christ-centered charities in your area and begin to do some research. Visit their websites, talk to their staff and learn the mission of each. For those that you find interesting, schedule a tour of their facilities where you can meet the staff and learn about the needs of the organization and volunteer opportunities. Finally, try one out on a short-term basis, maybe serving a meal at a homeless shelter or doing a work project at church. Involve your small group and visit local missions or invite guest speakers to discuss various volunteer opportunities.

A Volunteer or a Career

Remember, we each have our own calling in life. For some it may mean resigning your current position and becoming a missionary or pastor, or working for a ministry. For most, however, it will not mean leaving your employment and your income source for providing for your family. God needs believers in the marketplace to demonstrate integrity, high ethical standards and genuine love for coworkers. Your career may bring you much joy as you live out your calling using the talents God gave you.

God also needs His people to make companies profitable and take care of employees and their families. Some of the most joyful Christians see their employment as a way to care for their families and give them an opportunity to invest in their church and other local or global missions. Those that have received a calling to leave their career for full-time mission work are trusting that those in the marketplace, who have been blessed to earn income, will support them financially. How would your church be able to support your pastor and staff or give to local and global missions if it were not for the tithes and offerings of those serving in the marketplace?

Many laborers in the marketplace find that they are called to additional service outside of their career. They receive joy when they mentor a child away from work, or have a Bible study at the prison, or teach Sunday school. They're more complete, fulfilled and better at their job when they take the time to love others away from work. If you don't feel fulfilled in your current employment, before you resign to find your calling, start volunteering at your church or local mission.

If you still feel like you are to leave your place of employment, don't be surprised if a paid position opens up at the place you are volunteering. From a church or ministry perspective, usually the best candidates for a position are from the volunteer base who have shown their heart to love others in their service without getting paid for it. Also, remember that most paid ministry positions are administrative in nature, allowing volunteers the opportunity to serve others as they are called.

How God Looks at Callings

Don't mistake one calling as being higher than another in God's eyes. God doesn't see it that way. The apostle Paul writes to the church in Corinth, *"So neither he who plants nor he who waters is anything, but only God, who makes things grow. The man who plants and the man who waters have one purpose, and each will be rewarded according to his own labor. For we are God's fellow workers; you are God's field, God's building."* *(1 Corinthians 3:7-9)* Your goal is to find your calling in life, not to make

The joy that you will experience is not based on your results—how many come to Christ, how much money you can raise, or any other criteria. It is solely based on being obedient to God's calling in your life.

sure yours appears more spiritual or grandiose than another's. The joy that you will experience is not based on your results—how many come to Christ, how much money you can raise, or any other criteria. It is solely based on being obedient to God's calling in your life.

Finally, some of God's most obedient servants are those who have put their life on hold sacrificing greatly to care for an elderly parent, a disabled child or others in need. Parents raising children have one of life's biggest callings assigned to them. Don't sacrifice one calling for another. Maybe God is asking you to do more, but He may be asking you to wait. Be patient, and don't miss the joy as you serve alongside Jesus in your current responsibilities. Undoubtedly, your service is a sweet offering when presented at the throne of God.

"I strive more and more to be closer to God and receive more from Him so I can pour out more. Serving can be hard, but if you know that you're doing what God asks of you, His grace will be there."

Selansia Crawford (Bible study small group leader for at-risk teens)

PART 2

1) Since your first small group meeting, has the Holy Spirit been leading you to make changes in your life and pursue your calling? If so, what emotions have surfaced from this?

_____

_____

_____

_____

_____

2) What have you learned from this chapter that is helpful in discovering your calling?

_____

_____

_____

_____

_____

_____

_____

_____

_____

3) What steps do you feel God is leading you to take to discover how He wants to use you for His purpose?

_____

_____

_____

_____

4) For those that are currently experiencing the joy of fulfilling their calling, describe the importance of your relationship with God and the growth of your faith in carrying out your work.

_____

_____

_____

_____

5) With your group, discuss opportunities you are aware of in your church or at a local mission. What other opportunities are available for you to explore? Consider a group outing to visit some ministries you're interested in. Inquire as to what opportunities are there for you to serve as a group.

_____

_____

_____

_____

_____

_____

discussion questions continued on pg 24

6) *Imagine for a minute that someone gave you $1 million with the stipulation that you had to give it all away. Where would you give the money? This is a good indication of the people God has given you a heart to serve.*

_____

_____

_____

_____

_____

_____

7) *What if someone offered you your current wage or salary to do any work you wanted? What would you do? Again, where you would serve is a good indicator of the people he wants you to love.*

_____

_____

_____

_____

_____

_____

_____

_____

Part 3

Getting Out of the Boat

You're probably familiar with the story of Jesus' disciples traveling alone in a boat when suddenly Jesus appears to them walking on water. Of course, it's Peter who asks Jesus if he can join him. With Jesus' approval, Peter takes the leap of faith and does the impossible by walking on the water; that is, until he starts to doubt, which results in him sinking like an anchor. However, Jesus is there to quickly rescue him. *(Matthew 14:22-32)*

Life's biggest joys occur when we step out in faith. It is only then that we realize that the God of this universe is true to His promises. For a believer, nothing this side of heaven can compare to the awe and reverence we experience when God intervenes in our life. Maybe it's a healing or an answered prayer or some victory against all odds. When we step out in faith, we see that God is always true to His word. It's an absolute. The lesson we gain is that our faith is real, and God can be trusted. This is the platform from which God will involve us in His Kingdom work.

Again, look at Peter. Jesus filled Peter's nets with fish when he was first called. Then there was the walking on the water; the healings he witnessed; the feeding of the five thousand, then the four thousand; bringing Lazarus back from the dead and countless other encounters, many recorded in the gospel accounts. Finally, after the resurrection, when Peter fished all day

> Peter left his fishing boat for good on the shore; he gave up what he knew for the unknown. When it comes down to it, you will have to take a leap of faith. It's the only way.

and caught nothing, Jesus filled his nets again when He appeared to the disciples on the shore. *(John 21:6)* The result was that Peter was never the same. His faith had grown to the level that imprisonment, beatings and even death would not deter him from sharing the gospel of our risen Lord. His joy was indescribable, and he wouldn't even think of going back to fishing. His life had purpose.

Do you feel like you've been fishing all day and haven't caught a thing in your life? Do you dread Monday morning and another day of fishing? Peter left his fishing boat for good on the shore; he gave up what he knew for the unknown. When it comes down to it, you will have to take a leap of faith. It's the only way. Do I give up my Wednesday nights for a whole year to mentor youth in confirmation classes? Do I take my hard-earned vacation time and the money I've saved and use it to rebuild a home for a family in Haiti? Will God really take care of me in retirement if I start giving away the nest egg that I worked my whole life to build up? You will never know the answers to questions like these until you try it. It gets back to your eulogy. What is God calling you to do that will make an eternal difference?

"Having the opportunity to impact lives for eternity through my volunteer work has allowed me to see God working in ways that I had never seen before, deepened my faith, and also provided me with joy in seeing lives transformed by the gospel of Jesus Christ."

Blake Kruger (Analyst, State of Iowa, mentor/tutor for inner-city middle school students)

If you've been serious about finding your calling, you've noticed that you've been thinking about it a lot more. You've been more fervent in your prayers and have been searching the scriptures for a word from God. Maybe even memorized a few verses. You have investigated some ministry opportunities out there and have narrowed the list down to some that serve those you feel called to help. You may not have any answers, but God has your heart ready to start serving somewhere. You just want to love Jesus and love others. That's a good sign God is working in your life.

Think about what interests you. What news events are you drawn to when reading the paper or surfing the web? Maybe you want to help someone who's experiencing what you've encountered in your life. Your testimony of overcoming a trauma or addiction could be exactly what God has prepared you to share with a hurting world. What do you like to do that you could share with someone who's never had the opportunity? In every community there are neglected children who long for someone to teach them to cook, work on a bicycle or build a birdhouse. It could be the start of a relationship that changes the course of a youth's life. How many of our abandoned children can't break the cycle of poverty, substance abuse or

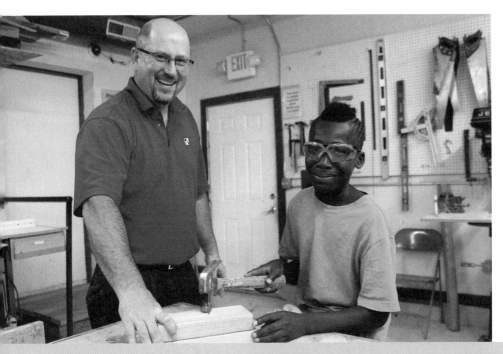

incarcerations in their family because no one ever loved them?

When God shows you what to do, you'll know it. It will excite you, and you will be drawn to it. It may take some time before you know, but if you seek after God's heart, you will be rewarded. Remember, through prayer and reading His Word our faith grows, and we are equipped for service. Some assignments require more preparation than others. Keep trying different things, on a short-term basis, until you find the thing that feels right.

Humility

When you feel like you've found the pearl, when your marching orders are clear, you'll do anything that needs to be done within your skill set. If God is drawing you to His service somewhere and you see how you can share Christ's love for a cause that has captured your heart, it doesn't really matter where you start. The key is that you get started.

Examine closely the motives of your heart. Your heart should be humble, as Christ's was, not seeking glory or recognition. *(Phillipians 2:6-11)* Your assignment may start out in one area and move to another. Your stature in the workplace should have no bearing on what you choose to do. If a homeless shelter's biggest immediate need is that the floor needs to be mopped, why wouldn't a CEO of a company love others by mopping the floor? The joy could be enormous. Sounds a lot like the King of Kings, the One whom all authority in heaven and on earth has been granted, washing the dirty feet of His disciples.

Maybe for you it's not the right time to jump out of the boat. You have ambitions of leading a discipleship class or Bible study at church, but you're raising children with busy schedules. Have you thought about writing your pastor or other church staff member an encouraging note? Could you help your pastor or church leader by making a few phone calls from home? Maybe you want to do prison ministry someday. Could you start by becoming a pen pal to an inmate or even getting a few names to include in your prayers? Maybe these groups could use your financial assistance to carry out their work. Contact the chaplain at the county jail or state correctional facility to see what's available.

PART 3

1) Share with your group what ideas God may be giving you about starting to serve or supporting a ministry financially. Is it apparent that God has given each member of your group a unique calling and spiritual gifts to meet so many different needs in the world?

_____

_____

_____

_____

_____

_____

2) If you have visited a ministry, researched other opportunities, or invited mission leaders to speak, discuss your findings with the group. Do you see opportunities that may be suited to you or other members of your group?

_____

_____

_____

_____

_____

_____

_____

3) If God has showed you your calling, where to invest your time or resources, share with the group how He showed you. What caused you to feel certain that God led you to this particular cause? Has God equipped you or given you financial resources to carry out your calling?

_____

_____

_____

_____

_____

_____

_____

4) If you're still searching, make a list of people to call at your church or other organizations to learn more about their needs.

_____

_____

_____

_____

_____

_____

_____

_____

_____

Part 4

A Life of
Service

If you're still exploring options and building your relationship with God, you're probably eager to get started. Don't give up. God may be preparing you for something beyond anything you've imagined. When you find it, you will see that it was worth the wait. Make sure you are spending time in your prayer closet; otherwise you will be frustrated and confused. God is willing to wait as long as it takes to build that intimate relationship with you. If you jump into a volunteer commitment without seeking God's heart first, you will find yourself ill-equipped, losing interest or burned out.

Maybe you've tried some one-time service projects and are excited to go back. God may have showed you things while serving, and now He wants you to take the next step. Making a long-term commitment (at least a year) to your church or other organization should not be taken lightly. The organization will be depending on you to do a great job with a joyful heart. If you're serving directly with others building relationships, such as mentoring or teaching a class, those you are serving will quickly notice whether your heart is in it. If you leave early, they may experience feelings of rejection or abandonment. This can be very damaging, especially to children living in broken families or those who have faced rejection their whole life.

Of course, God creates different seasons in our lives and may call us to many different things over our lifetime. It's important to make sure volunteer opportunities have a beginning and ending date. That way you can reevaluate at the conclusion whether God has another opportunity for you, or you are eager to continue where you left off. If your church or other organization does not have an ending date set for a specific assignment, you should ask them to set one. If the people you are serving know that there is a set date for the conclusion of your work, you will not disappoint them when it concludes. Obviously, many callings will allow you to build special relationships that you will not want to leave. And the organization will be eager to sign you up for another term. This is a good indication that you are receiving as much joy from the relationships you've built as those you are serving.

Your gifts of resources to charities may also change. God may call you to redirect funding to other needs, or you may be experiencing difficult times financially. Maybe you no longer feel compelled to support a specific cause within your church, outside of your tithe. Discontinuing or reducing funding, to any organization or missionary, like works of service, can cause feelings of rejection, especially if you have built a relationship with the organization's staff members. Don't let false assumptions create division or hurt feelings. Be open and honest about your change in financial giving. If you have concerns that need to be addressed, are not able to give financially, or believe God is telling you to give elsewhere, let those who have been counting on your support know. Your words of encouragement will dispel any feelings of rejection.

Dealing with High Expectations

Many of you, undoubtedly, have dealt with the frustration of a poor volunteer experience. You showed up to work and no one was there, the materials weren't available, or the people you were to serve didn't show. Maybe things were disorganized or you didn't feel properly trained.

Whatever your expectations are before you start, you should leave them at the door when you arrive. You shouldn't waste your time (or money) with a mission that is not true to what they portray. But, don't draw any conclusions right away. A youth worker who seems unfriendly may have just dealt with a discipline issue before you walked in. The foreman at the job site may have had trouble with the old ministry truck that caused him to be late. The chaplain at the jail may have been called away just as you were to arrive. The enemy does not want you there and will do everything in his power to dissuade you from continuing.

Other disappointments are no fault of the church or organization. You walked into your church to help hand out clothes to the homeless and found that they were unappreciative and demanding. The youth you were supposed to mentor stood you up…for the third time in a row! The inner-city teenagers snickered at you when you walked in the room. Nobody paid attention to your Bible study at the nursing home; in fact, most were sleeping!

These types of instances are exactly why God had you in your prayer closet before He called you out and why He longs for you to continue seeking Him in prayer. Your shattered expectations are God's reminder that He is the potter and you are the clay. *(Isaiah 64:8)* He will make absolutely sure that you realize it has to be Him working through you, not you working in your own strength. Perseverance is critical. The people you serve often test you to see the motives of your heart. If you quit early, they'll know you weren't real. They are saving themselves the pain of rejection and disappointment. Did you lash back? They'll assume you must not have the Jesus they're being told about.

A servant's heart should expect nothing in return. If you're looking at a tally of saved souls, how many students you tutored passed math, or whether you won the popularity contest among the volunteers, you're sure to experience disappointment. The fruit of your ministry is up to God alone. Jesus explained it this way:

"This is what the Kingdom of God is like. A man scatters seed on the ground. Night and day, whether he sleeps or gets up, the seed sprouts and grows, though he does not know how. All by itself the soil produces grain—first the stalk, then the head, then the full kernel in the head." (Mark 4:26-28)

God doesn't judge our obedience by what we produce; only that we get out in the field and plant the seed.

You may never know this side of heaven the impact your work has had on the Kingdom. You plant the seed but have nothing to do with how or when it sprouts and grows. This should be good news to you. The pressure's off. God doesn't judge our obedience by what we produce; only that we get out in the field and plant the seed.

Again, this is where the faith that you have been building in your quiet time is put into action. Your joy will come from being obedient to the Father, not by the outcomes your work produces. You may labor for weeks or months and see no signs of progress. Your work or financial gifts may go unnoticed by others or without any appreciation from staff. Good! God sees what is done in secret and promises to reward you. *(Matthew 6:4)*

Stay the course. Keep fighting the good fight God has laid out for you. God is not going to give you an assignment and then change His mind. Whether you realize it or not, your perseverance is an inspiration to the staff and other volunteers of the organization you serve. Ministry is hard work, consuming, and thankless. When you least expect it, you will get that phone call or letter thanking you for being the light of Christ in someone's life. God will allow you to catch a glimpse of heaven when the girl you've loved decides to give her baby up for adoption rather than abort, when your orphan boy walks across the stage at graduation or when you see the prisoner you visited show up in church with his family. The reward will be sweeter than anything you have experienced.

None of us will know the full impact we had on others serving our Lord Jesus; that is, this side of heaven. Even if your eulogy is read exactly as you wrote it, it will be nothing compared to the day you go home and see how God orchestrated your time, money and prayers to bring a lost world to Him. Many you loved will be there to greet you, and the sweetest words of all will be from Jesus, *"Well done good and faithful servant. Come and share your master's happiness." (Matthew 25:21)*

"Everyone I know who chooses to put their faith into action is changed. Their faith is strengthened, their hearts are softened, their conduct is improved, they approach life's challenges differently and are acutely aware of and appreciate the blessings of the Lord daily. They are more joyful and more peaceful. They love so deeply and unconditionally."

Allison Sullivan (Veterinarian, Bible study small group leader for inner-city teenage girls)

PART 4

1) Describe with your group any bad volunteer experiences you've had (without mentioning names of organizations). Did you work through the experience, or did it end abruptly?

_____

_____

_____

_____

_____

_____

_____

2) Have your expectations been detrimental to a successful volunteer experience? Would you do things differently now?

_____

_____

_____

_____

_____

_____

_____

3) Have you served or given resources to an organization long-term and subsequently discontinued? Describe why you departed and how you handled it. Would you do anything different now?

_____

_____

_____

_____

_____

4) How do you deal with feelings of rejection, being unappreciated or even unwanted when ministering to others? Did you give up on them too early?

_____

_____

_____

_____

5) Think about the day you go home to see Jesus. Does it motivate you to live your life any differently? What will you change?

_____

_____

_____

_____

_____

MANY YOU LOVED WILL BE
THERE TO GREET YOU, AND
THE SWEETEST WORDS OF ALL
WILL BE FROM JESUS,

"Well done **GOOD** and
FAITHFUL servant. Come and
share your master's happiness."

Matthew 25:21